The Monkey Movie Review

The Monkey Movie Review: An In-Depth Analysis of Stephen King's Latest Horror Thriller

Dennis Himmel

Copyright © 2025 Dennis Himmel

Table of Contents

Chapter 1

Introduction

Overview of *The Monkey*

In the world of horror, there are few things as unsettling as the concept of an object—one that appears innocent—transforming into a harbinger of death. *The Monkey*, a spine-chilling film based on Stephen King's 1980 short story, brings this terrifying idea to life with a sense of dread that lingers long after the credits roll. Directed by Osgood Perkins, the film explores the unnerving power of a seemingly harmless toy—a wind-up monkey that plays its cymbals with an eerie, rhythmic clash. But this is no ordinary toy. It's an instrument of death, and every time the cymbals clang, someone dies.

The film follows twin brothers, Hal and Bill, as they reconnect with a dark chapter of their childhood. After years of running from the truth, they discover that the evil monkey that plagued their lives still holds a deadly grip over them. What begins as a childhood curiosity transforms into a battle for survival, as they face the sinister force they unwittingly unleashed.

The Monkey takes the classic horror trope of an inanimate object turning monstrous and elevates it into a nightmarish journey, filled with tension, twists, and gut-wrenching suspense. But it's not just about scares—it's about the impact of trauma, the lingering presence of evil, and the consequences of trying to outrun the past. Perkins' direction combined with King's haunting storytelling creates a film that forces the audience to confront the idea that sometimes, there's no escaping the horrors we bring into our lives, no matter how hard we try.

The Legacy of Stephen King in Horror Cinema

Stephen King is undoubtedly one of the most influential figures in the horror genre, with his works forming the foundation for countless films, TV shows, and literary adaptations. From *Carrie* to *It*, King has redefined what it means to craft a truly terrifying narrative. His works delve into the darkest corners of the human psyche, often blending the supernatural with deeply emotional themes. This is what makes his stories resonate—there's a human element that grounds the horror, making it feel both personal and universal.

The Monkey is no different. While the premise of a toy monkey with deadly consequences may seem like a simple, albeit unsettling, idea, King's short story uses this eerie object to explore much larger themes. King has a unique ability to make the supernatural feel real, and *The Monkey* is no exception. The toy's power to kill isn't merely physical—it's psychological, rooted in the fear of the unknown and the trauma of the past. The monkey is a symbol of guilt, a reminder that we can never truly escape our darkest memories.

As with many of King's works, the horror in *The Monkey* is more than just the fear of a deadly toy; it's about confronting the emotional and psychological toll of living with fear, shame, and unresolved trauma. For those familiar with King's vast body of work, *The Monkey* fits seamlessly into his broader exploration of evil forces lurking just beneath the surface of ordinary life.

The Creative Team Behind the Film

Behind the haunting atmosphere and twisted narrative of *The Monkey* is a powerhouse creative team, led by director Osgood Perkins. Known for his work in atmospheric horror, Perkins brings a refined touch to the genre, creating films that aren't just about scares, but about the subtle, creeping terror that builds with each passing moment. His previous films, such as *The Blackcoat's Daughter* and *I Am the Pretty Thing That Lives in the House*, showcase his knack for crafting films that linger in your mind long after the screen goes dark.

In *The Monkey*, Perkins leans into the eerie, unsettling nature of King's original story, bringing a sense of claustrophobic tension to the film. The pacing is deliberate, allowing the horror to build slowly, wrapping around the viewer until it's inescapable. Perkins' direction ensures that every scene contributes to the sense of dread, from the chilling visual of the toy monkey's cymbals clashing to the gut-wrenching deaths that follow. His ability to balance psychological horror with visceral terror is evident in every frame, and it's this balance that makes *The Monkey* such an effective and memorable film.

Adding to the film's gravitas is the involvement of James Wan, one of the most successful horror filmmakers of the 21st century. Known for his work on the *Saw* franchise and *The Conjuring* films, Wan brings his unique expertise to the project as a producer. His involvement adds an extra layer of intensity and quality, ensuring that *The Monkey* adheres to the high standards of contemporary horror.

Wan's influence is especially evident in the film's atmosphere. Like many of his past works,

The Monkey plays on tension and the fear of what might happen next, rather than relying solely on shock value. The film's slow build-up allows the horror to seep into the audience's consciousness, creating a sustained sense of unease that intensifies as the story progresses.

Another key player in the film's success is the casting of Theo James, who plays the twin brothers Hal and Bill. James, known for his roles in *The Divergent Series* and *The White Lotus*, brings both vulnerability and strength to his dual role. The complexity of the twin brothers—one who is eager to confront their past and the other who wants to bury it—requires an actor capable of capturing these conflicting emotions. James' performance anchors the film, allowing the audience to connect with the brothers' internal struggle, even as they face the external terror of the evil toy monkey.

Supporting James are Tatiana Maslany and Elijah Wood, both of whom bring depth to their roles. Maslany, famous for her role in

Orphan Black, plays a crucial part in the unraveling of the mystery surrounding the toy. Wood, known for his iconic role in *The Lord of the Rings*, adds his unique touch to the narrative, bringing a sense of urgency and tension that propels the film forward.

With such a talented and experienced team at the helm, it's no surprise that *The Monkey* is shaping up to be a standout entry in the horror genre. Perkins' direction, combined with the creative contributions of Wan and the strong performances from the cast, ensure that *The Monkey* will not only be a faithful adaptation of King's story but also a film that will resonate with both horror fans and casual viewers alike.

As *The Monkey* prepares to take audiences on a terrifying journey, it's clear that the film is more than just another supernatural thriller. It's a film that explores the lasting impact of trauma, the terror of facing the past, and the chilling realization that sometimes, the things we fear the most are the things we can't escape. With Osgood Perkins' direction, Stephen

King's eerie story, and a talented cast, *The Monkey* is poised to be a must-watch for horror fans in 2025.

Chapter 2

The Plot Unfolds

The Sinister Toy Monkey: A Childhood Discovery

It all begins with a simple toy—a wind-up monkey with cymbals in its hands. At first glance, it seems harmless, even quaint. It's an object you might find tucked away in an antique shop, gathering dust on a shelf. But *The Monkey* is far from a harmless relic. In the hands of twin brothers Hal and Bill, this seemingly innocent toy becomes a malevolent force that will shape the course of their lives.

As children, Hal and Bill first encounter the toy in a seemingly innocuous moment—during a family yard sale. The toy, which once belonged to their father, is there among the other forgotten possessions. It's the kind of item you might ignore without a second thought, the kind of object most people would consider a relic of the past. But when the toy monkey's cymbals begin to clash, something unsettling occurs. The deaths begin. At first, it's subtle. A neighbor. A family friend. But soon, the pattern becomes undeniable: each time the toy monkey plays its eerie, rhythmic tune, someone dies. The brothers, too young to fully comprehend the terror of what's happening, do everything in their power to stop it. They try to burn it, throw it away, and even bury it deep in the woods. But no matter what they do, the toy always returns.

In this early part of the plot, the film expertly builds a sense of dread. The toy is the source of evil, yet its true nature is shrouded in mystery. The question lingers: is it truly the toy, or is there something else at play? Is there an ancient curse tied to this seemingly innocent object, or does the toy simply bring out the worst in the world around it? The brothers' growing awareness of the danger surrounding the toy monkey is both chilling and heartbreaking, as they find themselves unable to escape its lethal influence.

The Return of the Evil Monkey: Mysterious Deaths

As the brothers grow older and go their separate ways, they hope to leave the toy and its curse behind them. However, fate has other plans. The deaths that began when they were children return in full force. Years after they've tried to move on, the toy monkey—seemingly forgotten—resurfaces, bringing with it a wave of death and destruction.

When Hal receives a phone call informing him of yet another mysterious death, he's immediately reminded of his childhood nightmare. The toy, once again, has begun its deadly symphony. The characters who die are not always immediately connected to the brothers, but the deaths always follow a pattern: each one happens shortly after the monkey's cymbals clash.

In this part of the plot, the horror is no longer confined to a single family but extends to those around Hal and Bill. The sinister power of the toy doesn't care who it claims—it's relentless. The brothers, now adults, are pulled back into the nightmare they thought they'd escaped. The sense of helplessness is palpable as they realize that no matter how far they run, the toy monkey will always find them.

The death toll continues to rise, each victim's demise more grisly than the last. The deaths aren't just random, either. Each one feels personal. It's clear that whoever encounters the toy monkey becomes its next victim, whether they're family, friends, or strangers. The sense of danger builds as the brothers realize they can no longer ignore the evil that's once again awakened.

As the plot thickens, so too does the tension. The toy monkey, with its unsettling mechanical clanging, becomes more than just an object—it becomes an omnipresent force, ever on the verge of death, and ever eager to strike. For the audience, the realization sinks in that this is no ordinary killer. The toy monkey's power seems boundless. The brothers must confront the fact that the object they once believed was a simple childhood toy is not just a relic—it is an unstoppable force of death.

Hal and Bill's Mission to Destroy the Curse

In an effort to stop the toy monkey's curse, Hal and Bill decide to confront the source of the evil head-on. But the more they try to destroy it, the more they realize that they're not dealing with something that can be easily vanquished. The toy monkey is more than a mere object—it's a malevolent entity, a force that seems almost supernatural in nature. Each attempt they make to rid themselves of it only brings them closer to the dark truth: the toy isn't simply a cursed object; it's a manifestation of something far darker.

The brothers' mission becomes one of desperation. They scour their memories, looking for clues that might explain why the toy monkey is so deadly. They turn to their father's past, hoping to uncover something that might help them understand how the toy came to be so evil. As the brothers investigate, they uncover a disturbing truth: the toy monkey was not always a harmless trinket. There's a history behind it, one that stretches back generations.

The deeper the brothers dive into the mystery, the more they realize the full extent of the curse they're dealing with. This is no ordinary haunted object. The toy monkey is connected to an ancient evil, one that has been passed down through generations. As they come closer to understanding the true nature of the toy, the brothers are faced with a shocking revelation: the monkey isn't just killing anyone it encounters—it's targeting those who are connected to their family.

The film takes on a more existential tone as the brothers grapple with the horror of the situation. They realize that there's no easy solution. The toy monkey, despite all their efforts, can't be destroyed in the traditional sense. It is bound by an ancient and powerful force that won't allow it to be vanquished easily. The brothers' struggle to destroy the toy becomes a race against time. Every moment spent trying to find a solution is another moment that the toy is free to wreak havoc.

Their mission isn't just about destroying the toy; it's about saving themselves, their family, and anyone else who might fall victim to the monkey's deadly influence. As they piece together the puzzle of the toy's origins, the plot becomes more complex, and the stakes higher. The brothers must make difficult choices—choices that will not only determine their fate but also the fate of everyone they hold dear.

The final act of the film sees Hal and Bill confronting the toy monkey in a final showdown. This is the culmination of all the fear, tension, and mystery that has built up over the course of the film. The brothers must face the reality that there may be no way to escape the toy's curse. The ending leaves audiences with a sense of finality, but also with lingering questions about whether true evil can ever be truly eradicated, or if it always finds a way to return.

Chapter 3

The Characters and Performances

Hal and Bill: The Twin Brothers Haunted by the Past

At the core of *The Monkey* lies the complex dynamic between twin brothers Hal and Bill, portrayed by actor Theo James. The film delves into the emotional and psychological toll the toy monkey's curse has taken on their lives. Hal and Bill, though connected by blood, are not mere reflections of one another—they are shaped by their distinct responses to trauma and their struggle to overcome the horrors that have plagued them since childhood.

Hal is the more introspective of the two brothers. As a child, he was quick to recognize the dangers of the toy monkey, even before the full extent of its malevolent power was apparent. As an adult, Hal remains burdened by the weight of his past, often showing signs of guilt and regret for his inability to protect his family from the toy's fatal influence. His journey throughout the film is one of emotional reckoning. The horrors he experiences force him to face his unresolved trauma, and Theo James brings a raw vulnerability to the character. He portrays Hal's internal conflict with nuance, balancing moments of determination with vulnerability, creating a character whose struggle feels both personal and universal.

Bill, on the other hand, is more outwardly cynical and practical. While Hal is consumed by guilt, Bill is focused on finding solutions. Bill's approach to the curse is more action-oriented, a response that stems from his desire to regain control over a life that has continually been overshadowed by the toy monkey's influence. He is often the voice of reason in their adult lives, urging Hal to face the evil head-on rather than retreat. However, as the story progresses, Bill is also forced to confront the fact that no matter how hard he tries, the toy monkey's evil cannot be defeated by sheer will alone. Theo James portrays Bill with a sense of stoicism, yet his performance also allows glimpses of vulnerability, especially as the weight of their past catches up with him.

The chemistry between Theo James' portrayal of both brothers is essential to the film's emotional depth. Despite their differences, the bond between Hal and Bill is undeniable. The audience can sense the love, frustration, and unresolved tension that exists between the two, and their shared trauma becomes a driving force in their quest to rid themselves of the curse.

Tatiana Maslany: A Key Ally in the Brothers' Battle

Joining the cast is **Tatiana Maslany**, who plays a pivotal role as a key ally to the brothers. Maslany, known for her versatile performances in *Orphan Black* and *She-Hulk: Attorney at Law*, brings a level of complexity to her character that elevates the story. Her character is not only a supportive figure for Hal and Bill, but also someone who brings her own expertise to the battle against the toy monkey.

Maslany's character is introduced as an outsider who gradually becomes entangled in the brothers' struggle. Her initial skepticism gives way to full-fledged involvement as she witnesses the horror first-hand. What sets her apart is the fact that she's not merely a passive character; rather, she actively participates in the search for answers. She pushes the brothers to consider alternative explanations and approaches to the curse, becoming a necessary catalyst in their pursuit of resolution. Maslany brings her characteristic intensity and intelligence to the role, offering a grounded and practical counterbalance to the brothers' emotional turmoil.

As the plot thickens, Maslany's character serves as a reminder that the brothers cannot face this evil alone. Her involvement demonstrates the importance of support, solidarity, and trust in the face of an insurmountable challenge. Her performance enriches the film, providing a much-needed anchor amidst the chaos that surrounds the brothers.

Elijah Wood: The Enigmatic Character Who Holds the Key

No horror film would be complete without a character who provides essential information or guidance—someone who, though not necessarily involved in the primary conflict, plays a critical role in the unfolding mystery. In *The Monkey*, that character is played by **Elijah Wood**.

Wood, famous for his portrayal of Frodo Baggins in *The Lord of the Rings*, brings his trademark quirky energy to the role. However, in this film, his performance is far more subdued and mysterious. Wood's character is a former acquaintance of the brothers, one who knows something about the toy monkey's past that the brothers don't. His involvement in the story is enigmatic at first, but as the narrative unfolds, it becomes clear that he holds the key to understanding the true nature of the toy.

Elijah Wood excels at playing characters who are a bit offbeat, and here, he uses that skill to great effect. His presence in the film adds an element of unease. At first, the audience is unsure whether his character is genuinely helpful or whether he has his own hidden motives. Wood's ability to blend warmth with a slight sense of mystery enhances the character's role in the story. As the film progresses, it becomes clear that his character's knowledge is crucial to Hal and Bill's ultimate survival, but his involvement raises more questions than it answers, leaving the audience to wonder how much he truly understands about the evil they are confronting.

Supporting Cast: Adding Layers to the Narrative

In addition to the central trio of Hal, Bill, and their ally, *The Monkey* also features a strong supporting cast that enriches the narrative and adds layers to the film's overall tension. **Laura Mennell, Christian Convery,** and **Sarah Levy** deliver notable performances in smaller roles that contribute to the film's growing sense of unease. Mennell, known for *Project Blue Book,* plays a character who becomes entangled in the curse's web, adding to the mounting dread that surrounds the brothers. Convery, whose breakout role was in *Sweet Tooth,* plays a character whose death marks a key turning point in the plot. And Levy, famous for her role in *Schitt's Creek,* provides a brief but memorable turn as a character whose fate is directly tied to the toy monkey's curse.

Each of these characters plays a role in expanding the scope of the film's central conflict. While Hal and Bill are the emotional core of the story, the supporting cast helps to build the atmosphere of fear and unease that permeates the film.

The Importance of Performance in Horror Cinema

In horror films, the success of the narrative often hinges on the strength of the performances. The actors must sell the fear, the desperation, and the urgency of the situation. In *The Monkey*, the performances of Theo James, Tatiana Maslany, Elijah Wood, and the supporting cast are what transform the plot from a simple tale of a haunted toy into a gripping exploration of trauma, family, and survival.

Each actor brings a unique perspective to their character, making them more than just archetypes. Hal and Bill are not merely victims of a curse—they are deeply flawed individuals whose personal struggles mirror the external horror they face. Maslany's character is more than a mere ally—she's a necessary force that challenges the brothers' beliefs and pushes them toward action. Elijah Wood's mysterious figure adds an air of intrigue and suspense, while the supporting cast's roles emphasize the widespread reach of the toy monkey's evil influence.

In the end, it is the combination of these performances that makes *The Monkey* a compelling experience. The actors' ability to convey fear, grief, and determination creates an emotional connection with the audience. The horror in *The Monkey* isn't just in the terrifying events that unfold—it's in the characters' emotional journeys, making the film not just a thrilling ride, but a deeply human story of loss, love, and survival.

Chapter 4

The Director and Crew

Osgood Perkins: The Mastermind Behind the Horror

At the heart of *The Monkey* lies the directorial vision of **Osgood Perkins,** a filmmaker whose previous work has established him as a distinctive voice in modern horror. Known for his unique approach to atmospheric tension and psychological horror, Perkins brings his signature style to this chilling adaptation of Stephen King's 1980 short story. His direction is not only about creating jumps and scares but about crafting an eerie mood that lingers long after the credits roll.

Perkins is no stranger to the genre. His previous films—*The Blackcoat's Daughter*, *I Am the Pretty Thing That Lives in the House*, and *Longlegs*—showcase his aptitude for building dread through subtlety and psychological depth. In *The Monkey*, he builds on this foundation, drawing the audience into a narrative that is both unsettling and complex. Rather than relying on a heavy reliance on gore, Perkins manipulates the atmosphere to create a persistent sense of unease.

One of Perkins' most notable strengths as a director is his ability to create an atmosphere where the horror feels invasive, even when it's not overtly displayed. He often leaves the terror to the imagination of the viewer, using sound, lighting, and pacing to build suspense. In *The Monkey*, Perkins takes the seemingly innocuous premise of a toy monkey and transforms it into a symbol of something much darker, an evil presence that looms over the characters.

Through his careful direction, Perkins is able to evoke a psychological horror that works on multiple levels. The toy monkey, a once-innocent object, becomes a vehicle for deep-seated fears and unresolved trauma. Perkins crafts scenes that are at once haunting and thought-provoking, allowing the horror to stem not just from the supernatural elements, but from the emotional toll the curse takes on Hal, Bill, and the people around them.

A Vision of Horror Rooted in Humanity

What makes Perkins' direction stand out is his ability to keep the human element central to the horror. While *The Monkey* is filled with supernatural terror, the real fear lies in the characters' reactions to it and the way it forces them to confront their deepest fears and past regrets. Perkins understands that true horror is psychological—it's the emotional and mental unraveling of his characters that creates the deepest sense of dread.

His direction brings an intense focus on the inner turmoil of Hal and Bill, using the haunting presence of the toy to explore themes of guilt, grief, and redemption. As the brothers struggle to escape the toy's curse, they must also grapple with the emotional scars it has left behind. In this way, Perkins doesn't just tell a scary story—he forces the audience to face the emotional terror that comes with a life steeped in tragedy and fear.

In terms of visual style, Perkins is known for his careful use of color, shadow, and framing to communicate mood. In *The Monkey*, the toy is not just an object of horror—it's a visual representation of the brothers' unresolved trauma. Perkins frames the toy in ways that emphasize its malevolence, creating a sense of danger even when it's out of sight. His use of tight shots and close-ups on the toy during key moments of the film amplifies the sense of dread it inspires. The monkey, with its unsettling yellow eyes and constant cymbal-clashing, becomes a symbol of the danger that lurks just beyond the brothers' grasp.

The Cinematographer: Crafting the Atmosphere of Fear

A key collaborator in bringing Perkins' vision to life is **the cinematographer**, whose role in establishing the visual tone of *The Monkey* is critical. The use of lighting and camera work is integral to building tension throughout the film. Through clever manipulation of shadows, the cinematographer creates an atmosphere of paranoia, keeping the audience on edge and uncertain of what's lurking in the darkness.

Lighting is used strategically to create a contrast between safety and danger. During scenes where the brothers are reminiscing about their childhood or trying to live ordinary lives, warm, soft lighting predominates, giving a sense of nostalgia and comfort. However, once the toy monkey's presence is felt, the lighting shifts—shadows stretch, and the color palette becomes colder, darker, evoking an oppressive atmosphere. The toy monkey's presence is often highlighted by a stark, unsettling light that draws attention to its inescapable evil. This careful interplay between lighting and shadow helps the viewer navigate the emotional and psychological terrain of the story.

The cinematography also utilizes close-ups and wide-angle shots to create a sense of intimacy and isolation. In moments of personal reflection, the camera lingers on the faces of Hal and Bill, allowing the audience to connect with their inner struggles. At other times, the camera pulls back, offering a wider perspective of their surroundings, emphasizing the isolation that the brothers experience in their fight against the curse.

The cinematographer's use of framing also plays a role in heightening the tension. In several scenes, the toy monkey is placed just outside of the frame, suggesting its constant presence even when it's not directly in view. This subtle technique leaves the audience feeling uneasy, as though danger is always just beyond reach.

Sound Design: Creating an Unease Beyond Sight

Sound is another crucial element in creating the oppressive atmosphere of *The Monkey*. A large part of the film's terror is derived from the sound design, which underscores the horror without needing to rely on visual cues alone. The iconic sound of the toy monkey's cymbals clashing—"jang, jang, jang"—becomes an auditory symbol of impending death. This repetitive, almost hypnotic sound serves to heighten the anxiety felt by the characters, signaling the arrival of danger before anything else occurs on screen.

The sound design also incorporates subtle ambient noises, such as the creaking of old wood or the wind howling through a desolate house, all of which contribute to the film's atmosphere of unease. These sounds, often subtle and in the background, create a constant tension, as though something dreadful is always on the verge of happening.

In addition, the film uses silence strategically to build suspense. The absence of sound in certain key moments—before a tragic event or during moments of quiet reflection—allows the audience to feel the weight of the silence, amplifying the horror that follows. The contrast between the deafening clashing of cymbals and moments of silence creates a dynamic soundscape that draws the viewer deeper into the film's emotional and psychological intensity.

The Producers and Crew: Bringing the Vision to Life

Behind every successful film is a team of skilled producers and crew members who ensure that the director's vision is realized. *The Monkey* benefits from the collaboration of a talented production team that includes producers with a deep understanding of the horror genre and how to create a truly chilling experience for audiences.

The film's producers, working alongside Perkins, carefully orchestrated the film's production design, ensuring that the atmosphere of dread was consistent throughout. Every detail, from the look of the toy monkey to the design of the settings, was chosen to evoke a sense of foreboding. The production design team meticulously crafted the environments in which the brothers confront their fears, emphasizing isolation and the passage of time.

Additionally, the makeup and special effects teams worked to create the unsettling visual representations of death that haunt the characters, contributing to the film's sense of unease. While much of the horror in *The Monkey* is psychological, the practical effects used to depict death and decay are vital in ensuring the film remains grounded in a terrifying reality.

The Role of the Crew in the Final Product

Ultimately, *The Monkey* is a testament to the effectiveness of collaborative filmmaking. Osgood Perkins' vision as a director is brought to life by the combined talents of the cinematographer, sound designer, production team, and visual effects specialists. The crew's ability to work in unison ensures that every aspect of the film—from the haunting visuals to

the palpable atmosphere of dread—is cohesive
and impactful.

Chapter 5

Themes and Motifs

In *The Monkey*, horror transcends the mere presence of a malevolent toy. The film explores deep, timeless themes that resonate far beyond the realm of the supernatural. Through the cursed toy and the brothers' tragic journey, *The Monkey* delves into the delicate balance between childhood innocence and the terrifying forces of evil, the enduring grip of trauma, and the inescapable nature of death and fate. This chapter will explore these core themes and motifs that drive the narrative forward, adding layers of psychological depth to the story.

Childhood Innocence vs. Evil

One of the most striking contrasts in *The Monkey* is the interplay between the purity of childhood innocence and the corrupting influence of evil. At its core, the film is a tale of lost innocence, where something as innocent as a child's toy becomes the catalyst for horror. The toy monkey, with its cheerful cymbal-clashing sound, evokes memories of childhood play. However, this innocent symbol quickly transforms into a representation of something far darker—a force that not only threatens the brothers' lives but also distorts their memories of a time when life seemed carefree and full of possibility.

The presence of the toy in Hal and Bill's childhood home stands as a stark reminder of how evil can seep into the most innocent places, leaving a permanent mark. What was once a playful object becomes the harbinger of death, a symbol of a world that has lost its innocence. This contrast plays a crucial role in the film's emotional weight. Hal and Bill's attempts to outrun the curse of the toy monkey are not just physical—they're emotional. The toy forces them to confront their lost childhood, now forever marred by a malevolent force they cannot seem to escape.

The transformation of the toy from harmless to horrific encapsulates the shift from childhood innocence to the harsh realities of adulthood. *The Monkey* uses this shift as a metaphor for the way life's darker truths often intrude upon our most innocent moments, leaving behind emotional scars that can never fully heal.

This theme of innocence lost is woven into the narrative in the brothers' constant struggle to reclaim a semblance of peace. As children, they had no understanding of the toy's true nature. They saw it simply as a thing—an object that could be played with, a part of their world. But as adults, the toy is a constant reminder of the evil lurking beneath the surface of their memories. What was once a harmless artifact of their youth is now an inescapable terror, one that threatens not only their lives but also their sense of identity.

Trauma and the Past's Grip on the Present

Central to *The Monkey* is the theme of trauma—both the trauma inflicted by the toy monkey's presence and the personal trauma carried by Hal and Bill from their childhood. The film's horror is not only supernatural; it is psychological. As the brothers attempt to distance themselves from their past, they find themselves continuously drawn back into the nightmare that began with the toy monkey. This recurrence of trauma mirrors the way past experiences often shape our present realities, even when we try to escape them.

The film explores how trauma, particularly the trauma of childhood, doesn't simply fade away as time passes. Instead, it takes on a life of its own, affecting the brothers' relationships, their mental health, and their ability to function in the present. As Hal and Bill are forced to confront the curse once again, they must also face the emotional baggage they have carried for years. They cannot outrun their past—no matter how much they try. The trauma of losing loved ones, the sense of helplessness as children, and the guilt of feeling responsible for the evil unleashed all continue to haunt them.

The idea of trauma's grip on the present is exemplified in the brothers' attempts to move forward with their lives. Every time they try to break free from the toy monkey's curse, the past resurfaces to remind them of its hold. This is most evident in the film's eerie flashbacks, where the brothers relive moments from their childhood. These flashbacks are not mere recollections—they are living, breathing manifestations of the trauma that defines their existence. The past is not just something that happened; it is something that continually reasserts itself in the present.

In *The Monkey*, trauma is not only psychological—it is also physical. The brothers' bodies bear the marks of the toy's curse, both literally and figuratively. As the deaths continue, Hal and Bill are forced to face the consequences of the past, realizing that the trauma they thought they had buried can never truly be escaped. The film's exploration of trauma highlights how our past experiences shape our perceptions, our actions, and our understanding of the world. In the case of the brothers, their past will always return to haunt them, no matter how hard they try to outrun it.

The Concept of Death and Fate in Horror

Another central theme in *The Monkey* is the exploration of death and fate, particularly within the context of horror. The film constantly asks questions about the inevitability of death and whether fate is something we can control or something that is imposed upon us. From the very first instance of the toy monkey causing a death, the film establishes that death is not a random event but something that is orchestrated by the malevolent force tied to the toy.

The idea of death being manipulated by an external force is a motif that recurs throughout the film. The toy monkey's ability to summon death with the simple act of clashing its cymbals makes death seem not only inevitable but almost predestined. No one who comes into contact with the toy is safe, and the film repeatedly shows that the curse of the toy monkey is inescapable, no matter what the characters do. This sense of fatalism imbues the film with a haunting atmosphere, as viewers are left questioning whether the characters can ever truly escape their fate.

Death in *The Monkey* is not portrayed as a peaceful release but as a violent and unnatural force. The toy monkey's victims are subjected to brutal, unexplained deaths, emphasizing the randomness and cruelty of fate. However, as the film progresses, the idea of fate becomes more complex. Hal and Bill are not passive victims—they actively seek to change their fates by confronting the toy. Their attempts to destroy it represent their struggle to break free from the fatalistic grip of the curse.

This theme of fate versus free will is a hallmark of the horror genre, where characters often find themselves trapped in situations that feel beyond their control. In *The Monkey*, fate seems unavoidable, but the brothers' decision to fight back against it speaks to the human desire to take control over the uncontrollable. Even in the face of an insurmountable evil, the brothers cling to the hope that they can change the course of their lives. Whether they succeed or fail in this endeavor, however, is a question that remains unanswered until the very end of the film.

Death as a Constant Presence

Death is not just a plot device in *The Monkey*— it is an ever-present force that shapes the narrative. The repeated deaths tied to the toy serve as a constant reminder of the inevitability of death, which is a theme often explored in horror films. But *The Monkey* goes further by linking death to the idea of fate and destiny. The deaths that occur in the film seem not only random but also bound to a cosmic order, suggesting that the characters' fates are sealed by forces they cannot comprehend.

In the end, *The Monkey* offers no simple answers to the question of death. It suggests that while we may struggle against the forces that seek to control our lives, death remains an unchanging certainty. The film leaves the audience with a lingering question: are we ever truly in control of our fate, or are we simply bound to a predetermined path?

In conclusion, *The Monkey* is more than just a supernatural horror film. It is a complex exploration of childhood innocence, trauma, and the inevitability of death. Through its chilling narrative and deeply human themes, the film taps into universal fears, making it not just a story about a toy monkey but a reflection on the human condition itself. The horror in *The Monkey* does not come only from the toy but from the emotional and psychological toll it exacts on the characters. As the brothers struggle to break free from the curse, they are forced to confront the deepest, most terrifying aspects of themselves—tragedies from their past and the inescapable reality of their fate.

Chapter 6

Cinematic Design

Cinematic design plays a pivotal role in *The Monkey*, transforming what could be a conventional horror film into an immersive, unsettling experience. Every visual element, from the haunting production design to the nuanced cinematography, enhances the story's chilling atmosphere. Additionally, the iconic toy monkey is not just a symbol of evil—it is intricately woven into the film's design, carrying both visual and symbolic weight. This chapter delves into the careful craft behind the film's cinematic design, examining how each aspect contributes to the horror, atmosphere, and thematic depth of *The Monkey*.

Production Design: Crafting the Eerie Atmosphere

The production design of *The Monkey* is crucial in establishing the film's chilling tone. From the very first moments, the sets evoke a sense of unease and discomfort. The filmmakers have painstakingly crafted each location to reflect the oppressive nature of the curse that haunts the brothers, Hal and Bill. The houses, the rooms, and the spaces they inhabit are all saturated with a sense of decay and abandonment, as if they themselves are living relics of a traumatic past. This setting provides a stark backdrop for the supernatural events that unfold, emphasizing the inescapable grip of the toy monkey on the brothers' lives.

The interiors of Hal and Bill's childhood home, for example, are designed with muted, faded colors that suggest a place where memories are trapped—frozen in time by the sinister presence of the toy. The homes they live in as adults mirror this sense of stagnation. The spaces are filled with old furniture, cluttered rooms, and dim lighting that all contribute to a sense of decay, further echoing the emotional and psychological rot left by their shared traumatic experiences. The film's production design focuses on creating an atmosphere that feels haunted—not by ghosts in the traditional sense, but by memories, guilt, and a malevolent force.

The rooms themselves often feel cramped and claustrophobic, enhancing the tension as the brothers attempt to escape the toy monkey's curse. The narrow hallways, the outdated furniture, and the general disrepair of the environment subtly reflect the brothers' own emotional state: trapped in a past they cannot outrun. The careful attention to detail in the design of these spaces allows the film to create an atmosphere where every corner seems to hold something sinister, every shadow feels alive with malevolent intent.

Furthermore, the use of mirrors and reflective surfaces is prevalent throughout the film, symbolizing how Hal and Bill are haunted by their past. These reflective surfaces often show distorted or warped versions of reality, suggesting that the brothers are not only physically trapped in the spaces they inhabit but also mentally ensnared by the curse. This motif of distorted reflections becomes a key part of the film's production design, reinforcing the theme that the brothers are living in a nightmare from which there is no escape.

Cinematography Techniques that Enhance Horror

In *The Monkey,* cinematography is not merely a tool for capturing the action—it is an integral part of building the film's tension and sense of dread. The camera work in the film is designed to place the viewer in a state of unease, enhancing the horror through its strategic use of angles, lighting, and movement. The film employs various techniques to make the audience feel trapped within the brothers' world, amplifying the horror at every turn.

One of the most striking techniques used in *The Monkey* is the manipulation of space through framing. The cinematography often isolates the characters within the frame, emphasizing their vulnerability and isolation. In moments of heightened tension, the camera pulls back to reveal vast, empty spaces, creating a sense of abandonment and hopelessness. The brothers are often shown as small figures against these expansive backdrops, underscoring their powerlessness in the face of the overwhelming evil that surrounds them.

The use of shadows and lighting is another key element in the film's visual language. Dimly lit scenes, where shadows crawl across the walls, create an atmosphere of creeping dread. The filmmakers use these shadows to disorient the viewer, making them feel as though something is always lurking just out of sight. This is particularly effective in scenes where the toy monkey is involved, as the camera often highlights the toy in stark, unnerving contrast to its surroundings. The eerie glow of the toy's eyes or the rhythmic sound of its cymbals seem to pierce through the darkness, as if the toy itself is a malevolent force that bends the environment to its will.

The camera also frequently employs tight, close-up shots during moments of horror. These shots focus on the characters' faces, capturing their fear and internal struggle. The intense close-ups draw the audience into the characters' psychological turmoil, making them feel like they are experiencing the terror firsthand. This technique is particularly effective in conveying the psychological horror of the film, where the brothers' fear is as much about what is happening in their minds as it is about the external threat.

Another notable cinematographic technique is the use of shaky cam during moments of chaos or panic. This movement amplifies the sense of confusion and desperation that the brothers feel, further heightening the emotional impact of the film. The erratic camera movements reflect the characters' sense of losing control over their circumstances, making the audience feel just as unsettled as the brothers themselves.

The Iconic Toy Monkey: Visual and Symbolic Impact

The toy monkey in *The Monkey* is not just a physical object; it is an icon of evil and the driving force behind the horror in the film. Its design—an antique wind-up toy with cymbals— is deceptively simple at first glance. However, as the story unfolds, the toy takes on a greater significance, symbolizing the intrusion of evil into the innocence of childhood and the inescapability of fate.

Visually, the toy monkey's appearance is striking. Its mechanical movements, which seem almost too lifelike, are unsettling in their repetition. The sound of the cymbals clashing together—jang, jang, jang—becomes a horrifying motif throughout the film, an auditory cue that signals death. The toy's eyes, often depicted as unnervingly lifeless and hollow, seem to follow the characters, creating an illusion of sentience. This eerie gaze underscores the idea that the toy is more than just an object; it is a malevolent force that is fully aware of the destruction it causes.

Symbolically, the toy monkey represents the loss of innocence. It is a relic from the brothers' childhood, a reminder of a time when life seemed simple and safe. However, the moment the toy is introduced into their lives, it disrupts that safety, transforming the brothers' memories of their childhood into something nightmarish. The toy monkey is not just a trigger for the supernatural events that unfold; it is a physical manifestation of the curse that plagues the brothers. Its presence represents the inescapable grip of the past and the trauma that continues to haunt them.

The toy is also a symbol of the uncontrollable nature of death and fate. The rhythmic clashing of its cymbals is a constant reminder that death is never far away—always just a sound away. The toy's ability to cause death with such a simple, mechanical action reflects the randomness and inevitability of the curse.

The toy becomes a symbol of fate's indifference, a force that cannot be fought or reasoned with. As the brothers attempt to destroy the toy, they come to realize that they are powerless in the face of this malevolent force, highlighting the film's exploration of death and destiny.

Conclusion

Cinematic design in *The Monkey* is not just an aesthetic choice—it is an essential part of the storytelling. Through its production design, cinematography, and the visual symbolism of the toy monkey, the film crafts a deeply immersive and unsettling atmosphere. The visual elements serve to heighten the horror, amplifying the psychological and emotional stakes of the narrative. The toy monkey, as both an object and a symbol, encapsulates the themes of childhood innocence lost, trauma that cannot be outrun, and the inevitability of death. In every frame, *The Monkey* reminds the viewer that the terror is not just what lurks in the shadows but what lingers in the past—waiting to strike again.

Chapter 7

Horror Elements

The Monkey expertly blends various subgenres of horror to create a suspense-filled, heart-pounding experience. While supernatural forces certainly play a role in the narrative, the film's psychological depth adds an unsettling layer of tension. This chapter explores the key horror elements that make *The Monkey* such a powerful addition to the genre, including its blend of supernatural and psychological horror, the reimagining of a classic horror trope through the toy monkey, and the way the film builds and maintains suspense to keep audiences on edge.

The Supernatural vs. Psychological Horror

At its core, *The Monkey* is a haunting exploration of the boundaries between the supernatural and psychological terror. The toy monkey itself is an unambiguously supernatural object—a cursed item that wreaks havoc on the brothers' lives, causing death and despair. However, the film doesn't rely solely on supernatural shock tactics. It also delves deeply into psychological horror, exploring how the brothers' past trauma, guilt, and unresolved fears feed into their descent into madness as they confront the curse.

The supernatural aspects of the film—manifested in the malevolent toy monkey—are stark and unrelenting. The object seems to operate according to its own dark logic, unleashing chaos with every mechanical clang of its cymbals. It embodies the kind of unstoppable evil often seen in traditional horror films, but what sets *The Monkey* apart is how it plays with the characters' psychological states. While the brothers' minds are clearly under siege by the curse, the film leaves the audience wondering whether the supernatural occurrences are truly happening or if they are a manifestation of the brothers' collective trauma.

This psychological element gives the film a sense of ambiguity that heightens the horror. The viewer is not always sure whether Hal and Bill are witnessing real, supernatural events or if their deteriorating mental states have made them more susceptible to paranoia and hallucinations. In this way, *The Monkey* keeps the audience in a state of uncertainty, blending the supernatural with the very real horrors of psychological disintegration.

For instance, as Hal and Bill begin to unravel, their actions become increasingly erratic, and they start questioning their own sanity. Their decisions, which might initially seem rational, begin to mirror the disjointed logic of someone spiraling into madness. Is the monkey truly the source of their destruction, or is it the reflection of their fractured minds? This question runs through the film, adding a level of psychological depth that enriches the horror, making the supernatural element feel even more menacing.

The Monkey: A Classic Horror Trope Reimagined

At its heart, *The Monkey* plays with a familiar horror trope: the cursed object. From haunted dolls to vengeful relics, the idea of a seemingly innocent object harboring malevolent power has been a staple of horror for decades. *The Monkey* takes this well-worn concept and reimagines it, giving the cursed object—an old, wind-up toy monkey—an unnervingly fresh take.

The toy monkey itself, at first glance, is an unassuming and even somewhat nostalgic artifact. Its small brass cymbals, its tattered fur, and its creaking mechanical movements evoke memories of simpler times, a time before the brothers' lives were torn apart by the deaths associated with it. However, this veneer of innocence is shattered the moment the toy starts its rhythmic clang—jang, jang, jang—and death follows.

The toy monkey's symbolic role in *The Monkey* speaks to one of the most primal fears in horror: the fear of the inanimate, the fear of the object that moves or acts on its own. Here, the toy is not merely a mechanical device; it is an instrument of death, one that acts with malicious intent. This inversion of a child's toy, traditionally a symbol of innocence and comfort, creates a deeply unsettling effect. The monkey is a reminder that evil can often hide in the most benign of places, turning the everyday into a source of terror.

The filmmakers elevate this horror trope by making the toy an ongoing presence, one that seems to have a life of its own. It's not just a relic of the past; it's a ticking time bomb, ready to spring its deadly consequences at any moment. Each time the toy clatters its cymbals, it signals a death that is inevitable—an uncontrollable chain of events. The monkey, in this sense, becomes not only a physical object but also a symbol of fate—death is coming, and there's nothing anyone can do to stop it.

What makes *The Monkey* so effective is that the film doesn't rely on traditional jump scares or supernatural creatures lurking in the shadows. Instead, it uses the toy monkey as a tool to explore the idea of fate, of something so simple yet so deadly that it completely upends the characters' lives. The terror here is not just in the object itself, but in the inevitability of death that it represents.

Deaths and Suspense: Keeping the Audience on Edge

A critical element of horror is suspense, and *The Monkey* masterfully builds tension throughout the film by keeping the audience on edge. The deaths in the movie are not mere spectacles; they serve to increase the stakes, deepen the psychological horror, and heighten the tension with every passing moment.

One of the most compelling ways the film keeps the audience gripped is through its pacing. The deaths do not occur in quick succession, but rather they are spaced out just enough to build dread. Each death is followed by a period of uncertainty, where Hal and Bill try to rationalize what happened, questioning if it was really the toy monkey's doing or if something more sinister is at play. The uncertainty surrounding the toy's influence—combined with the brothers' emotional and psychological turmoil—creates a building sense of dread that permeates every scene.

The toy monkey's influence is always present in the background, but its full impact is not immediately apparent. The rhythm of its cymbals—the jangling sound—becomes a recurring motif, a harbinger of death that looms over the brothers and the audience. The toy doesn't simply appear and kill; it builds its malevolent presence slowly, becoming an inescapable part of the brothers' lives.

Suspense is also driven by the brothers' attempts to destroy the monkey. Every time they think they have rid themselves of it, it somehow reappears. The sense of futility and inevitability intensifies, and the audience begins to feel the same hopelessness that Hal and Bill are experiencing. The monkey is not just a tool for terror; it is a symbol of fate that the brothers cannot escape. This adds a layer of psychological horror, as the audience becomes increasingly unsure whether the deaths are truly caused by the toy or if they are simply the result of the brothers' growing desperation and mental collapse.

The deaths themselves are often shocking, but not in the traditional sense of horror films. They are not grotesque or graphic for the sake of shock value; instead, they are unsettling because they happen in quiet, almost mundane settings. The calm before the storm—where everything seems normal and safe—amplifies the horror when the toy monkey strikes. The tension builds as the brothers realize that no matter how hard they try, they can't outrun the death that the toy promises.

Another way the film keeps the audience on edge is through the unpredictable nature of the deaths. As the toy monkey has no clear pattern, viewers are kept guessing who will be next, and how it will unfold. This uncertainty is key in horror; it keeps audiences invested and constantly on the lookout for what might happen next.

Conclusion

The Monkey expertly blends supernatural and psychological horror, offering a fresh take on a classic horror trope while keeping the audience in suspense throughout. The toy monkey itself serves as a menacing symbol of fate, death, and the power of the past, while the film's pacing and unpredictable deaths enhance the tension. The film's strength lies not just in the supernatural elements but in its exploration of the psychological toll that trauma and guilt can take on the mind. Every death, every moment of suspense, pulls the audience deeper into the brothers' nightmare, leaving them uncertain and uneasy until the final, haunting moments.

Chapter 8

Critical Reception

As with any highly anticipated horror film, *The Monkey* was met with both excitement and scrutiny upon its release. Critics and audiences alike were eager to see how Osgood Perkins' direction, combined with the dark narrative drawn from Stephen King's chilling short story, would resonate. In this chapter, we delve into the first reactions and early reviews of *The Monkey*, comparing it to other horror films, and examining the overall impact it has had on both the genre and contemporary horror cinema.

First Reactions and Early Reviews

From the very first screenings, *The Monkey* garnered strong reactions—especially from horror enthusiasts who had long awaited a new adaptation of Stephen King's works. The fusion of King's eerie storytelling and Perkins' distinct atmospheric horror direction raised expectations for the film's release. The buzz surrounding the film built early on, driven by its unnerving premise, an all-star cast led by Theo James, and a strong association with the producer of *The Conjuring* and *Saw*, James Wan.

Upon its debut, reactions from both critics and audience members were mixed but leaned towards positive, with particular praise directed at the film's psychological tension and its ability to engage the audience on an emotional level. The film's slow-burn narrative and haunting atmosphere struck a chord with viewers who appreciated the more cerebral aspects of horror. Several reviews applauded the chilling portrayal of the toy monkey as a symbol of fate and evil, though some found the pacing to be somewhat deliberate. Critics pointed out that while the movie was certainly frightening, it was also a meditation on trauma and guilt, with these deeper layers enriching the horror rather than overwhelming it.

Some early reactions were especially positive about the performances. Theo James' portrayal of both Hal and Bill was praised for capturing the subtle differences between the brothers, making their emotional unraveling feel genuine. The supporting cast, including Tatiana Maslany and Elijah Wood, were also lauded for their dynamic performances, which helped ground the supernatural elements of the story in a more relatable, human context.

However, not all early reviews were glowing. A few critics found the pacing of the film a bit slow and mentioned that the supernatural elements felt familiar and perhaps too derivative of other King adaptations. A minority of viewers expressed disappointment that the horror didn't reach the fever pitch of more fast-paced thrillers. While many found the idea of the cursed toy intriguing, some wished for more overt scares or faster developments. Despite these critiques, the general consensus was that *The Monkey* successfully created a deep sense of unease and fear through atmosphere rather than cheap thrills.

Comparing The Monkey with Other Horror Films

The arrival of *The Monkey* at the height of a horror resurgence in cinema sparked comparisons to other popular films in the genre, particularly within the subgenres of supernatural and psychological horror. While *The Monkey* draws inspiration from classic horror tropes—the cursed object, supernatural retribution, and a battle with fate—its execution is distinct enough to set it apart from similar films.

One film that critics often mentioned in comparison to *The Monkey* was *The Babadook*, directed by Jennifer Kent. Both films deal with the psychological scars left by traumatic events and the lingering effects of those traumas on the characters' ability to move forward. Like *The Babadook*, *The Monkey* examines the thin line between the supernatural and psychological terror, drawing the audience into the characters' personal struggles as much as the horrors they face externally. Both films explore grief, guilt, and the sense of being haunted—not just by external forces but by the very emotions and memories that shape our reality.

Another key comparison was made with *It Follows*, the 2014 horror film directed by David Robert Mitchell. Both films rely on a slow-building, pervasive sense of dread rather than relying on fast-paced jump scares or slasher tropes. In *It Follows*, the entity relentlessly pursues its victims, just as the cursed monkey relentlessly haunts the lives of Hal and Bill. The eerie, unstoppable force that drives the horror in both films creates a sense of inevitability, where the characters' actions seem futile against the unrelenting threat.

That being said, *The Monkey* is notably different from many recent horror films that rely heavily on gore or shock value. Films like *Hereditary* or *Midsommar* also delve deeply into familial trauma, but their horror is more visceral, often showcasing disturbing images and intense emotional confrontations. *The Monkey*, by contrast, relies on an atmospheric approach, gradually building its terror with an unsettling, almost voyeuristic sense of dread that accumulates slowly.

Many critics and viewers praised *The Monkey* for its willingness to take a quieter, more meditative route through the genre. It's less about the immediate horror and more about creating a lasting sense of unease. Its similarities to other horror films help define its place within the genre, but its unique blend of supernatural elements, familial trauma, and psychological horror give it a signature style that differentiates it from other titles.

Critics' Thoughts on the Film's Impact

As the dust settled on its release, critics began reflecting on *The Monkey*'s place within the broader landscape of contemporary horror films. Many noted that the film is a testament to the ongoing evolution of the genre, especially in its ability to balance the supernatural with the deeply human aspects of fear and trauma. By focusing on the psychological unraveling of the two brothers as they face the horror of their past, the film presents a fresh take on how fear manifests within us and how trauma shapes our perception of reality.

Several critics highlighted the growing influence of filmmakers like Osgood Perkins, whose atmospheric and cerebral approach to horror has brought a new sensibility to the genre. Perkins, known for his previous work in films like *I Am the Pretty Thing That Lives in the House*, has built a reputation for crafting horror films that are more about psychological disintegration than mere shocks. His ability to create an aura of dread through silence, tension, and subtlety has earned him praise as one of the leading voices in modern horror filmmaking.

In terms of its cultural impact, *The Monkey* has also sparked discussions on the resurgence of classic horror tropes. While it doesn't break new ground in terms of plot structure or the basic ideas of cursed objects and revenge, it successfully reinvents these themes for a new generation of horror fans. The film's success indicates that there is still a hunger for thought-provoking, atmospheric horror that examines not just the supernatural, but the very human emotions that drive us toward fear and survival.

The film's legacy is still being shaped as more audiences watch and reflect on it, but there's no doubt that it has had a significant impact on how we think about horror today. By combining psychological depth with supernatural terror, it challenges viewers to look beyond the surface of what scares them and confront the deeper fears that lurk within.

Conclusion

The Monkey stands as a strong contender in the realm of supernatural and psychological horror, offering a rich narrative, nuanced performances, and a unique atmosphere that separates it from more typical genre fare. The early critical reception of the film was generally positive, with praise for its emotional depth, its psychological tension, and its slow-burn horror. While it certainly draws comparisons to other films in the genre, it ultimately stands out for its balance of supernatural terror and psychological complexity. The film's impact on the horror landscape is already being felt, with critics hailing it as one of the more sophisticated and unsettling entries in recent years.

With its thoughtful exploration of trauma, guilt, and fate, *The Monkey* proves that horror doesn't have to be loud or graphic to be effective. It's a film that lingers, and in that lingering presence, it finds its power. As it continues to receive critical attention, *The Monkey* will undoubtedly continue to spark conversation among horror fans, filmmakers, and critics alike.

Chapter 9

Stephen King's Influence

Stephen King's works have become a cornerstone of modern horror, not just in literature but also in film. The writer, often hailed as the "King of Horror," has seen many of his novels and short stories adapted for the screen, leaving a lasting imprint on the genre. His ability to craft deeply psychological horror, blended with elements of the supernatural and the mundane, has made his works a staple in cinematic adaptations. *The Monkey*, an adaptation of King's 1980 short story, continues this legacy, bringing his unique brand of terror to life in new and unsettling ways. In this chapter, we examine King's influence on the world of horror cinema, how his short stories have been adapted for the big screen, and what sets *The Monkey* apart from other King adaptations.

The Legacy of Stephen King in Film

Stephen King's influence on horror films cannot be overstated. His stories have been turned into some of the most iconic films in the genre, including *Carrie*, *The Shining*, *It*, *Misery*, and *Pet Sematary*. What sets King apart from many other horror writers is his focus not only on the supernatural but on the characters who must contend with these forces. His work often explores the vulnerabilities, fears, and inner conflicts of ordinary people, making the horror elements feel real and deeply personal.

King's ability to create relatable characters facing extraordinary circumstances has made his stories particularly effective in cinematic adaptations. His characters are often flawed, complex, and undergo significant emotional and psychological transformations. This focus on character depth has allowed filmmakers to craft films that resonate with audiences on multiple levels, combining elements of traditional horror with themes of human struggle, grief, and redemption.

The relationship between King's written work and its cinematic interpretations is a symbiotic one. While some adaptations have been met with mixed reception (such as *The Dark Tower*), others have become classics in their own right. Films like *The Shining* and *It* are still celebrated today for their ability to capture the essence of King's storytelling while translating it to the screen in ways that engage the audience's senses and emotions. King's stories offer rich material for filmmakers to explore, and his presence in the film industry is undeniable. His legacy is one of haunting characters, psychologically complex narratives, and supernatural terrors that feel all too real.

Adapting King's Short Stories to the Big Screen

While Stephen King is perhaps best known for his full-length novels, his short stories have also proven fertile ground for cinematic adaptation. Short stories allow filmmakers to focus on specific, often concentrated moments of horror, creating tense, high-stakes narratives that can leave a lasting impression in a relatively short amount of time. This is evident in adaptations such as *The Mist, 1408,* and *The Shawshank Redemption*—each of which takes a brief glimpse into a larger, emotionally charged world.

The Monkey falls into this tradition, adapting one of King's lesser-known but nonetheless disturbing short stories. The transition from the page to the screen, however, is never a simple process. King's short stories often require filmmakers to distill the core elements of the narrative—namely, the tension, the sense of impending doom, and the psychological horror—and translate them into visual and auditory cues that will unsettle viewers. This can be challenging, especially when the original story contains much of the horror in its subtlety, atmosphere, or internal conflicts rather than in overt action or terror.

What makes adapting King's short stories particularly compelling is the unique challenge of fitting them into a more traditional movie-length format. Short stories often lack the extended build-up that a novel can provide, meaning the filmmakers must work quickly to establish stakes, build characters, and evoke fear. In *The Monkey*, this challenge is met by creating a slow-burn narrative, with plenty of room for the unsettling atmosphere to develop. The eerie toy monkey, which acts as the focal point of the horror, slowly reveals its sinister influence over the brothers and their lives. Perkins, the director, opts for a methodical pace that allows tension to build in increments, rather than through rapid-fire shocks. This approach reflects King's own method of horror—slow, creeping, and insidious.

Many of King's short stories also share thematic similarities, particularly in their exploration of trauma, guilt, and the inescapability of past events. These themes are central to *The Monkey,* where the cursed toy acts as a symbol of the brothers' unresolved emotional turmoil. King's ability to tap into deep psychological fears and combine them with supernatural forces has been a hallmark of his writing and continues to influence his film adaptations. This is especially evident in *The Monkey,* where the terror of the toy monkey is less about the object itself and more about what it represents—the inescapable shadow of the past and the crushing weight of unresolved guilt.

What Makes The Monkey Stand Out Among King's Works

The Monkey might not be as famous as some of Stephen King's other works, but it is a remarkable entry in his expansive collection.

What sets it apart is its exploration of familial trauma and the way that it intertwines with supernatural horror. Unlike many of King's more widely known stories, which often focus on larger-scale threats (e.g., the shape-shifting clown Pennywise in *It* or the haunted hotel in *The Shining*), *The Monkey* is a more intimate and personal horror story. The brothers' struggle is not just against a physical threat but against their own psychological scars, creating a film that blends psychological horror with supernatural elements.

The toy monkey, which serves as both the catalyst for the horror and a symbol of past trauma, is also an interesting point of distinction. While cursed objects are a common trope in horror, the concept of a seemingly innocent, childlike toy as an agent of death is uniquely unsettling. This subversion of childhood innocence—an object typically associated with comfort and nostalgia—adds a layer of terror that is both psychological and emotional. The toy is not simply an inanimate object; it represents the brothers' inability to escape their past and the lingering specters of their childhood trauma.

Additionally, *The Monkey* stands out for its careful pacing and the way it blends character-driven drama with supernatural horror. The film doesn't rely on overt gore or flashy scares; instead, it uses atmosphere, character development, and tension-building to create a slow but persistent dread. King's short story, much like the film, is more interested in the emotional toll of the curse than in the physical consequences. The horror doesn't just come from the deaths that occur, but from the idea that no matter what the brothers do, they cannot escape their past or the consequences of their actions.

Furthermore, *The Monkey* is set apart by its themes of fate and guilt. Many of King's works delve into these themes, but in *The Monkey*, they are central to the plot. The brothers are not merely fighting for survival; they are fighting to free themselves from the chains of their past. This focus on fate and the inevitability of death adds a layer of existential horror that is not always present in King's more traditional horror stories, making it a unique and introspective exploration of the genre.

Conclusion

Stephen King's influence on horror filmmaking is immeasurable, and *The Monkey* serves as another testament to his impact. The film captures King's signature combination of supernatural horror and psychological depth, creating a story that resonates long after the credits roll. The adaptation of King's short stories has proven to be a rich field for filmmakers, and *The Monkey* stands as an exemplary adaptation of his work. Its focus on familial trauma, guilt, and fate sets it apart from other King adaptations, and its slow-burn, atmospheric horror is a nod to King's unique ability to tap into our deepest fears.

The Monkey proves that even lesser-known King works can have a lasting impact, both on horror fans and on the broader landscape of film. By blending supernatural terror with emotional depth, it continues the tradition of King's legacy, offering a haunting and unforgettable cinematic experience.

Chapter 10

Horror Through the Ages

Horror cinema, like all film genres, evolves over time, adapting to cultural shifts, technological advancements, and societal fears. The roots of horror are steeped in ancient folklore and mythology, where terror was conjured through tales of monsters, ghosts, and supernatural forces. As cinema emerged, horror found its voice in the dark corners of film, giving rise to countless subgenres, from gothic to slasher to supernatural horror. However, one of the most enduring and unsettling tropes in horror is the concept of the "evil object." From cursed dolls to haunted mirrors, these seemingly innocent items often serve as conduits for malevolent forces, embodying the terror of the unknown and the malevolent power that lurks behind everyday objects.

In this chapter, we take a look at the evolution of evil objects in horror cinema, exploring how this trope has been used to great effect over the years. We will also examine how *The Monkey* fits into the larger context of horror cinema, particularly through its use of the cursed toy monkey as both a symbol of childhood innocence and a harbinger of death.

Evil Objects in Horror Cinema: A Brief History

The idea of an object harboring evil is as old as folklore itself. Tales of cursed items or objects imbued with dark powers have been passed down for generations. In the early days of horror cinema, filmmakers tapped into this folklore, giving rise to a range of iconic films that explored the terror of malevolent objects. These objects could take many forms—haunted mirrors, dolls with sinister eyes, or even books with dark powers. The key to their effectiveness lies in their ability to turn the ordinary into the extraordinary, to take something familiar and transform it into a source of terror.

One of the earliest and most influential films to explore the concept of an evil object is *The Cabinet of Dr. Caligari* (1920). This silent German Expressionist film, often considered one of the greatest horror movies of all time, uses the "cabinet" as a central symbol of madness and control. While not an "object" in the traditional sense, the cabinet functions as a source of malevolent power, influencing the actions of the characters and creating a chilling atmosphere of fear and disorientation. This marked the beginning of horror's fascination with objects that were more than they appeared.

Throughout the mid-20th century, the evil object trope became a staple of horror cinema. Films like *The Curse of the Cat People* (1944) and *The Doll* (1946) introduced cursed dolls and objects that seemed innocuous at first, only to reveal their sinister nature. Dolls, in particular, became a favorite in horror due to their association with childhood and innocence, creating a stark contrast between the safety they should represent and the danger they harbor.

One of the most iconic evil objects in horror is, of course, the cursed mirror. *The Ring* (2002) and *Candyman* (1992) are two examples where mirrors serve as portals to otherworldly forces, leading to death and destruction. The reflection of the characters in these mirrors is not just a visual device but a manifestation of the evil that lurks beyond.

Another significant example is *The Evil Dead* (1981), where the Necronomicon, a cursed book, serves as the catalyst for the demonic terror that unfolds. The idea of an object having the power to summon evil forces or release destructive powers is central to this film, and it became a cornerstone of the horror genre in the years that followed.

In the 21st century, horror filmmakers have continued to explore the concept of cursed objects, often blending traditional elements with modern storytelling techniques. Movies like *Annabelle* (2014), centered around a haunted doll, and *The Conjuring* (2013), with its cursed artifacts, have reignited interest in the evil object trope, proving that this concept still has the power to unsettle and terrify audiences.

How The Monkey Fits into the Horror Genre

While *The Monkey* may not be the first film to explore the concept of a cursed object, its unique take on the trope sets it apart from others in the genre. The toy monkey at the center of the film is not just an object of evil—it is a symbol of unresolved childhood trauma and the inescapable grip of the past. In this way, *The Monkey* blends the supernatural elements of the cursed object with deeply emotional themes, creating a horror film that is both psychological and supernatural in nature.

The film's focus on a childhood toy as the central object of horror is a notable departure from many of the genre's other evil object films. While dolls, mirrors, and books have been explored extensively, *The Monkey* uses a seemingly innocent object—a wind-up toy monkey—to create a sense of dread. The toy, with its clanging cymbals and lifeless eyes, becomes a terrifying symbol of the brothers' unresolved guilt and trauma, as well as the unrelenting presence of death. This reimagining of a familiar object is part of what makes the film so unsettling.

The toy monkey itself is a perfect example of the *evil object* trope. At first glance, it appears harmless—perhaps even nostalgic—but it is this very innocence that makes its malevolent power all the more terrifying. Its ability to cause death and suffering with the simple act of clashing its cymbals taps into the primal fear of objects taking on a life of their own, an idea that is at the heart of many of the greatest horror films. Unlike other evil objects that might have overt supernatural qualities, the toy monkey in *The Monkey* has a quiet, almost passive presence—its power is not in how it moves or behaves, but in what it represents.

The evil object trope is often used to explore themes of control, fate, and the limits of human agency. In *The Monkey*, the brothers' inability to escape the curse of the toy monkey serves as a metaphor for the inescapability of their past actions. The toy, in a way, controls their fates, forcing them to confront their deepest fears and regrets. As they struggle to rid themselves of the toy, they realize that the true horror is not just in the deaths it causes, but in the way it forces them to reckon with their own emotional baggage.

Moreover, the use of the toy monkey as a symbol of childhood innocence gone awry adds another layer of psychological depth to the film. The idea that an object, once a source of joy and comfort, can become a source of terror is a powerful one. It plays on the universal fear of the loss of innocence, a theme that is central to many horror films. *The Monkey* takes this fear and amplifies it, turning the toy into a nightmarish presence that haunts the brothers' lives long after their childhood is over.

While *The Monkey* is not the first film to explore the cursed object trope, its treatment of the toy monkey as a symbol of guilt, trauma, and inevitable fate places it in a unique position within the horror genre. The film blends traditional supernatural horror with psychological drama, creating a horror experience that is both emotionally resonant and terrifying in its execution. In this way, *The Monkey* is a modern take on the classic horror trope, reimagining the evil object in a way that feels fresh and unsettling.

Conclusion

The evil object has been a central theme in horror cinema for decades, with filmmakers using everything from dolls to mirrors to books as vessels for terror. *The Monkey* fits squarely within this tradition, but it also pushes the boundaries of the trope by adding emotional and psychological depth. The toy monkey is more than just an evil object—it is a symbol of the brothers' unresolved trauma, guilt, and the inevitable grip of the past. By blending supernatural horror with emotional conflict, *The Monkey* reinvents the cursed object genre, offering a fresh take on a classic horror theme. As we move forward in this guide, we will continue to explore how *The Monkey* fits within the larger landscape of horror cinema and its place in the ongoing evolution of the genre.

Chapter 11

Behind the Scenes

Behind every great film lies a wealth of work, technical expertise, and creativity that bring the story to life. *The Monkey*, with its dark atmosphere and unsettling premise, is no exception. In this chapter, we pull back the curtain on the making of the film, exploring the filming locations, production insights, and the special effects that brought the sinister toy monkey to life. From set design to the use of cutting-edge technology, the production team worked tirelessly to craft an experience that would not only scare audiences but also leave them with a sense of unease long after the credits roll.

Filming Locations and Production Insights

The setting of *The Monkey* plays a significant role in establishing its eerie, foreboding atmosphere. The filmmakers chose locations that enhanced the psychological tension of the film, opting for a mix of realistic settings and atmospheric environments that would make the supernatural elements feel even more grounded. The majority of the film was shot on location in various parts of the United States, with a few key scenes filmed in more remote, isolated areas that were specifically selected to evoke the sense of desolation and impending doom.

The choice of filming locations reflects the thematic undercurrent of the film—how the past never truly leaves us, how memories, particularly those tied to childhood, linger in the darkest corners of our minds. The filmmakers chose a small, quiet town for many of the scenes involving the childhood home of Hal and Bill. This location served to highlight the contrast between the brothers' seemingly idyllic past and the horrors they are about to confront. The setting of their childhood home is both a place of nostalgia and terror, a perfect backdrop for a story about unresolved trauma and inescapable guilt.

In addition to the suburban settings, the film also features scenes in dark forests and desolate landscapes. These locations, bathed in twilight or shrouded in fog, help to build the sense of isolation and impending horror. The vast open spaces of nature become a kind of antagonist in themselves, amplifying the feelings of helplessness and vulnerability that the brothers experience as they seek to destroy the toy monkey. The visual contrasts between the familiar and the eerie environments play an important role in the horror, reminding the audience that danger can lurk in the most unexpected places.

Another key aspect of the film's production design was the careful attention to detail in creating the brothers' world. From their childhood bedrooms to the desolate locations they venture into as adults, every space is meticulously crafted to reflect the tension and emotional weight of their journey. Set designers worked closely with the director to ensure that every detail, from the placement of objects in the background to the lighting of each scene, contributed to the overall feeling of dread.

Filming also took place in several large soundstages, where many of the more controlled, suspenseful sequences were shot. Here, the filmmakers could control every element—from lighting to sound—ensuring that the supernatural elements, especially the toy monkey, would have the desired impact on the audience. The shift from outdoor locations to the studio environment allowed for more intimacy in the scenes, creating a sense of confinement and inevitability that helped heighten the tension.

While the locations themselves contributed heavily to the film's tone, the collaboration between the cast and crew also played a crucial role in bringing the story to life. Director Osgood Perkins worked closely with cinematographer Mike Gioulakis to create a visual language that would evoke the film's psychological horror elements. Together, they focused on creating a stark, haunting atmosphere through the use of low lighting, deep shadows, and elongated camera movements. The result is a film that feels both claustrophobic and expansive, as if the world is closing in on the brothers while they try desperately to escape the grip of the toy monkey.

Special Effects: Bringing the Toy Monkey to Life

One of the standout elements of *The Monkey* is the toy monkey itself. From its initial innocent appearance to its transformation into an agent of terror, the toy becomes one of the most crucial components of the film's horror. The filmmakers faced the challenge of making a simple, wind-up toy seem genuinely frightening. They used a combination of practical effects, CGI, and puppetry to ensure that the toy monkey was as unnerving as possible, making it both a physical and psychological presence on screen.

The toy monkey, which features cymbals that crash together with a disturbing clanging sound, was carefully designed to evoke both nostalgia and fear. Its appearance is intentionally creepy, with glassy, emotionless eyes and an unnaturally stiff posture. The puppet was created to be as lifelike as possible, with subtle movements that could make it seem like it was functioning under its own volition. Special effects artists, under the guidance of Perkins, worked with expert puppeteers to bring the toy to life on set, manipulating it in subtle ways that gave it an uncanny, almost sentient quality.

For scenes where the toy monkey needed to be more animated—such as when it crashes its cymbals or moves on its own—the filmmakers used CGI enhancements. However, the goal was always to make these effects feel seamless and grounded in reality. The CGI was designed to enhance the toy's actions without detracting from its physical presence. In these scenes, the toy monkey moves with an eerie precision, its mechanical movements becoming increasingly unsettling as the story progresses. The combination of practical effects and CGI made the toy feel real enough to elicit a genuine sense of dread from the audience, heightening the supernatural tension in each sequence.

The sound design for the toy monkey also played a crucial role in making it frightening. The constant, jarring sound of the cymbals crashing together became a signature of the toy's presence. To achieve the perfect sound, the sound design team experimented with a variety of cymbals, both real and artificial, until they found the right balance. The sound had to be loud enough to shock the audience but also eerie enough to linger in the background, creating a sense of unease even when the toy was not physically present.

In addition to the toy monkey itself, the filmmakers used special effects to create the gruesome deaths that occur in the film. Blood and gore are staples of many horror films, but *The Monkey* takes a more psychological approach to its horror, relying on the buildup of tension and the emotional stakes of the characters. Special effects artists worked meticulously to create deaths that felt both visceral and emotionally impactful. The effects were designed not just to shock but to convey the true horror of the brothers' struggle with their past and the curse that follows them.

The physicality of the deaths, combined with the psychological horror of the toy monkey's influence, added to the film's overall sense of dread. The filmmakers wanted the audience to feel the weight of each death as if it were a personal tragedy rather than a mere spectacle. By using a blend of practical effects, CGI, and expert sound design, *The Monkey* manages to bring the toy and the horrors it represents to life in a way that is both convincing and terrifying.

Conclusion

The behind-the-scenes process of *The Monkey* showcases the impressive teamwork and technical expertise required to bring the story to life. From the carefully chosen filming locations that heighten the film's sense of dread to the special effects that bring the toy monkey to life, every element of production was designed to enhance the psychological horror and emotional impact of the film. The filmmakers understood that horror is not just about what is seen on screen but also about the atmosphere, sound, and emotions evoked through every decision made in the creation of the film. The result is a horror experience that is deeply unsettling, both in its supernatural elements and its exploration of trauma and guilt.

Chapter 12

Release Information

The anticipation surrounding *The Monkey* has been steadily building, with fans of horror and Stephen King alike eagerly awaiting the release of this chilling adaptation. The film, directed by Osgood Perkins, is set to make a big splash in theaters across the world, and this chapter provides all the essential release information you need to mark your calendars and prepare for the spine-tingling ride that *The Monkey* promises to be.

Release Dates and Premiere Details

The Monkey is slated for an exclusive theatrical release, making it an event film that will be screened in select theaters globally. The official release date for the United States is set for **February 21, 2025.** This date marks the beginning of the film's theatrical run, where it will be shown in major cinemas and independent theaters across the country. With the film's increasing buzz and the involvement of major horror names like Stephen King, Osgood Perkins, and James Wan, fans can expect this to be one of the early horror highlights of 2025.

Before its nationwide release in the U.S., the film will have special early screenings and premieres in various international markets. **Spain** will be one of the first countries to screen the film, with a premiere set for **February 14, 2025,** in Madrid, followed by a **February 19, 2025** release in France. **Australia and Brazil** will both get the film on **February 20, 2025,** and other countries, including **Mexico, Poland,** and **Japan,** will follow soon after.

In addition to traditional theater screenings, *The Monkey* is expected to be featured in **limited release formats,** including special IMAX and premium large-format showings. These formats are perfect for fans looking to fully immerse themselves in the atmospheric horror of the film. The use of advanced sound and visual technologies in these formats will undoubtedly elevate the terror and suspense that the film has to offer.

The film's international releases will also see it being screened in select theaters in **Germany, Italy, Argentina,** and **Ecuador,** where it will be shown with subtitles to accommodate local audiences. While the film will be shown with its original English dialogue, the subtitled versions will ensure that *The Monkey* can reach a broader, global audience.

Where and How to Watch The Monkey

For those who prefer watching films from the comfort of their own homes, there is good news: *The Monkey* will eventually make its way to digital platforms, where it will be available for purchase or rental. While no official date has been confirmed for the digital release, fans can expect it to land on major streaming services after its theatrical run. These services may include **Amazon Prime Video, Apple TV, Google Play,** and **Vudu,** among others, allowing viewers to rent or buy the film for streaming at home.

The home video release of *The Monkey* will likely come with special features, such as director's commentary, behind-the-scenes documentaries, and deleted scenes, offering further insight into the making of the film. Horror enthusiasts and fans of the filmmakers' previous works will no doubt find these bonus materials intriguing, as they dive deeper into the creative process behind bringing this dark and twisted story to the screen.

For those looking for the ultimate cinematic experience, the film's Blu-ray and DVD versions will also be available for purchase. The physical release will feature stunning artwork, a detailed booklet, and additional content that will satisfy collectors and fans who want to keep a piece of the film in their libraries.

Global Reception and Early Buzz

Ahead of its release, *The Monkey* has already generated significant buzz in the horror community, with early reactions from those who've seen test screenings praising its atmospheric tension and the unsettling presence of the toy monkey itself. The film's eerie atmosphere, combined with strong performances from its talented cast, has people talking about it as a must-watch for horror fans in 2025. Given its association with Stephen King and the successful collaboration between director Osgood Perkins and producer James Wan, expectations are high for the film to become a standout entry in the horror genre.

It's also worth noting that horror films of this caliber often have a unique cultural resonance. *The Monkey*'s themes of childhood trauma, guilt, and the haunting persistence of the past are universal, making it a compelling watch for a diverse audience worldwide. Fans of both supernatural and psychological horror will find much to appreciate in this film, and early international reactions have indicated that the movie is poised to be a global hit, further adding to its buzz.

Conclusion

The Monkey is shaping up to be one of the most talked-about horror films of 2025, thanks to its chilling story, talented cast, and the expertise of director Osgood Perkins. With a release schedule that spans the globe, the film will have its premiere in select international markets starting in **February 2025**, followed by a wider release in theaters across the U.S. and beyond.

Whether you're planning to watch it on the big screen or stream it from the comfort of your own home, *The Monkey* promises to be an unforgettable experience for fans of psychological and supernatural horror. Mark your calendars for **February 21, 2025**, and get ready to face the terror of the toy monkey when it hits theaters near you.

Chapter 13

Conclusion

As the release date for *The Monkey* draws near, horror fans are in for an experience that promises to deliver on the eerie suspense and psychological dread that the genre is known for. With its strong connections to Stephen King's legacy, its unique take on the "evil object" trope, and a talented team both in front of and behind the camera, this film is poised to leave a lasting mark on the horror landscape. In this chapter, we'll explore why *The Monkey* deserves a spot on every horror fan's watchlist and offer some final thoughts on its potential impact on the future of horror cinema.

Why The Monkey Should Be on Every Horror Fan's Watchlist

In the world of horror cinema, few stories have the lasting power to haunt audiences like those told by Stephen King. With *The Monkey*, we witness another one of King's works come to life on the big screen, and this adaptation stands out not only because of its source material but also because of the fresh creative team involved. Directed by Osgood Perkins, the film takes a short story with a deceptively simple premise — a toy monkey that causes death — and builds it into a multi-layered, atmospheric horror experience.

At the core of the film is an exploration of trauma and the past, themes that King often revisits in his writing, and *The Monkey* is no exception. The brothers Hal and Bill, played by Theo James, are not just fighting against a cursed object; they are fighting against the ghosts of their own childhood, their guilt, and the trauma that has shaped their lives. This depth of emotional conflict adds a level of complexity to the film, making it more than just a simple horror flick. The audience is not merely being asked to witness a series of terrifying events; they are being invited to engage with the characters' emotional journeys, which are just as haunting as the supernatural forces at play.

What makes *The Monkey* particularly compelling is how it strikes a balance between psychological horror and supernatural terror. While the toy monkey and its mysterious deaths are undeniably chilling, much of the horror stems from the brothers' spiraling sense of guilt and helplessness. Perkins' direction ensures that the film maintains a constant sense of dread, whether it's the ominous ticking of the monkey's cymbals or the weight of the brothers' inability to escape their past. This combination of elements — the supernatural, the psychological, and the emotional — makes *The Monkey* stand out in a genre often dominated by predictable jump scares and formulaic plots.

With a talented cast, led by Theo James and supported by the likes of Tatiana Maslany and

Elijah Wood, the performances add another layer of realism to the film's otherwise surreal terror. The strength of the performances allows the audience to connect deeply with the characters, which only enhances the stakes when the horror begins to unfold.

Moreover, *The Monkey*'s visual design — from the chilling toy monkey itself to the film's overall aesthetic — further elevates the tension. Every element of the production is crafted to pull the viewer deeper into the world of the film, where the lines between the past and present blur, and no one is ever truly safe. Whether you're a fan of supernatural horror, psychological thrillers, or films that explore the deep scars left by trauma, *The Monkey* has something to offer, making it a must-watch for anyone who loves a good scare.

Final Thoughts on Its Impact and Future in Horror Cinema

The influence of *The Monkey* on horror cinema could extend far beyond its initial release. While the film is based on a short story by Stephen King, it taps into a universal fear that transcends the realm of fiction: the fear of being unable to escape the past. This emotional core, combined with its innovative approach to horror, positions *The Monkey* as a film that will likely be studied and admired by filmmakers, critics, and horror fans for years to come.

In terms of legacy, *The Monkey* could serve as a touchstone for future horror films that seek to combine psychological depth with supernatural elements. As the genre continues to evolve, the blend of trauma, guilt, and supernatural horror that Perkins and King explore here may inspire a new wave of filmmakers who want to delve into more complex emotional and psychological landscapes. The ability to create genuine, lasting fear in an audience doesn't rely solely on scares or gore, but rather on how well the story engages with deeper, more relatable fears. *The*

Monkey's potential to do just that could change how horror films are made, pushing the genre toward more nuanced, thought-provoking narratives.

On a broader scale, the film also marks the continuing relevance of Stephen King in the world of cinema. King's works have been adapted into some of the most iconic horror films in history, and *The Monkey* is no exception. However, this adaptation offers something new: a tighter, more personal focus on the emotional damage that lingers long after the supernatural events have ended. As King's legacy in horror cinema continues to grow, *The Monkey* may become one of his most memorable adaptations — a film that blends the best of old-school horror with modern sensibilities.

While *The Monkey*'s primary focus is on terror and the supernatural, its lasting impact may be more subtle. It's a film that forces the audience to confront the inevitability of death, the weight of past mistakes, and the desire for redemption. These are not just themes confined to the horror genre, but themes that resonate with anyone who has ever struggled with guilt or the specter of their past. In this sense, *The Monkey* could have a ripple effect beyond horror, touching on universal human experiences that transcend genre.

Conclusion

In conclusion, *The Monkey* is a film that horror fans should not miss. With its deep emotional core, masterful direction from Osgood Perkins, and standout performances from its talented cast, it offers a fresh take on the horror genre. The film's exploration of trauma, guilt, and the supernatural provides a complex narrative that elevates it beyond the typical horror flick, making it a compelling watch for both casual fans and genre aficionados alike.

As it takes its place within the wider world of horror cinema, *The Monkey* is poised to become a standout film that not only entertains but also challenges its viewers. The combination of Stephen King's source material, Perkins' unique vision, and the film's unforgettable atmosphere ensures that *The Monkey* will be talked about for years to come. Whether you're a long-time fan of King's work or simply a lover of well-crafted horror, this film deserves a spot on your watchlist.

Printed in Great Britain
by Amazon